LEARN GUJARATI

THE EASY WAY

WRITER

KASHNIL KHILOSIA

PRINTED BY OXUNIPRINT LIMITED

Illustrator - Maruti Entertainment
Designed by - Rajen Kotecha

Audio CD
Speaker of English version - Poonam Chauhan
Speaker of Gujarati version - Sanjay Kamdar
Recording studio - Taal

First published by Culture N Language in 2013.
Copyright © 2013, Culture N Language, United Kingdom.

A few words of encouragement from Honourable Shri Narendra Modi, Gujarat's Chief Minister.

Date: 24-01-2013

Bahen Shree Kashnil,

Very few people are blessed with capability of **turning adversity into opportunity.** Every life has some moments, which defines and changes the track of the life forever. It is hard to overcome a challenge. Instead of sitting back complaining about how situations are, it is essential to work on solutions to come out of it with broader aspect of benefiting others.

I convey my wishes to you especially your efforts to pen-down a book to benefit Gujarati Community, rather a generation at United Kingdom.

I wish you best for your endeavors.

(Narendra Modi)

To,
Shree Kashnil Khilosia.
Email: Kashnil@yahoo.co.uk

Narendra Modi
Chief Minister, Gujarat State

CONTENTS

- CHAPTER - 1. GUJARATI ALPHABET & VOWELS.   5
- CHAPTER - 2. PARTS OF THE BODY.   9
- CHAPTER - 3. MY FAMILY.   12
- CHAPTER - 4. MY HOUSE.   16
- CHAPTER - 5. 1 TO 10 NUMBERS.   22
- CHAPTER - 6. DAYS OF THE WEEK & TIME.   25
- CHAPTER - 7. COLOURS & SHAPES.   29
- CHAPTER - 8. RELIGION & FESTIVALS.   32
- CHAPTER - 9. VEGETABLES & FRUITS.   37
- CHAPTER - 10. INDIAN FOOD.   41
- CHAPTER - 11. ANIMALS & BIRDS.   44
- CHAPTER - 12. NATURE & WEATHER.   47
- CHAPTER - 13. OPPOSITES.   50
- CHAPTER - 14. DAILY ACTIONS.   54
- CHAPTER - 15. GUJARAT.   60
- ANSWER KEY.   62

Preface

The focus of this book is on speaking and listening, rather than writing or reading Gujarati. I would like you to work your way through this book in a relaxed and supportive atmosphere. This will enable you to enjoy learning the Gujarati culture and language. Practicing is the key to successfully learning any language and each chapter contains an exercise, which will help you evaluate and measure your progress.

Based on my experiences, I have found that many individuals of Gujarati origin who reside outside of India, were not familiar with authentic Gujarati. They also did not recognise all of the Gujarati alphabets, specifically letters such as Na – ણ and La – ળ, because there are no equivalent Engilsh alphabets. Hence, they tended to use R – ર as a substitute. So ladwu (fighting) would become Larwu. In this book, I have highlighted these occurrences in red text. Where there is no translation in red, this indicates that both translations are the same.

For Example:

(BLUE) English - Conventional Gujarati translation - Gujarati (Hair - Vaal - વાળ)

(RED) Modern Gujarati translations (Hair - Vaar - વાર)

Moreover, my listen and learn CR-ROM contains all pronunciations in clear phonetic tones to aide you in learning.

Do not forget to visit my website where you will find constantly updated additional learning material and you can also email me on kashnil@culture-language.com with your bouquets and brickbats.

Chapter - 1

GUJARATI BARAKSHRI - ગુજરાતી બારાક્ષરી

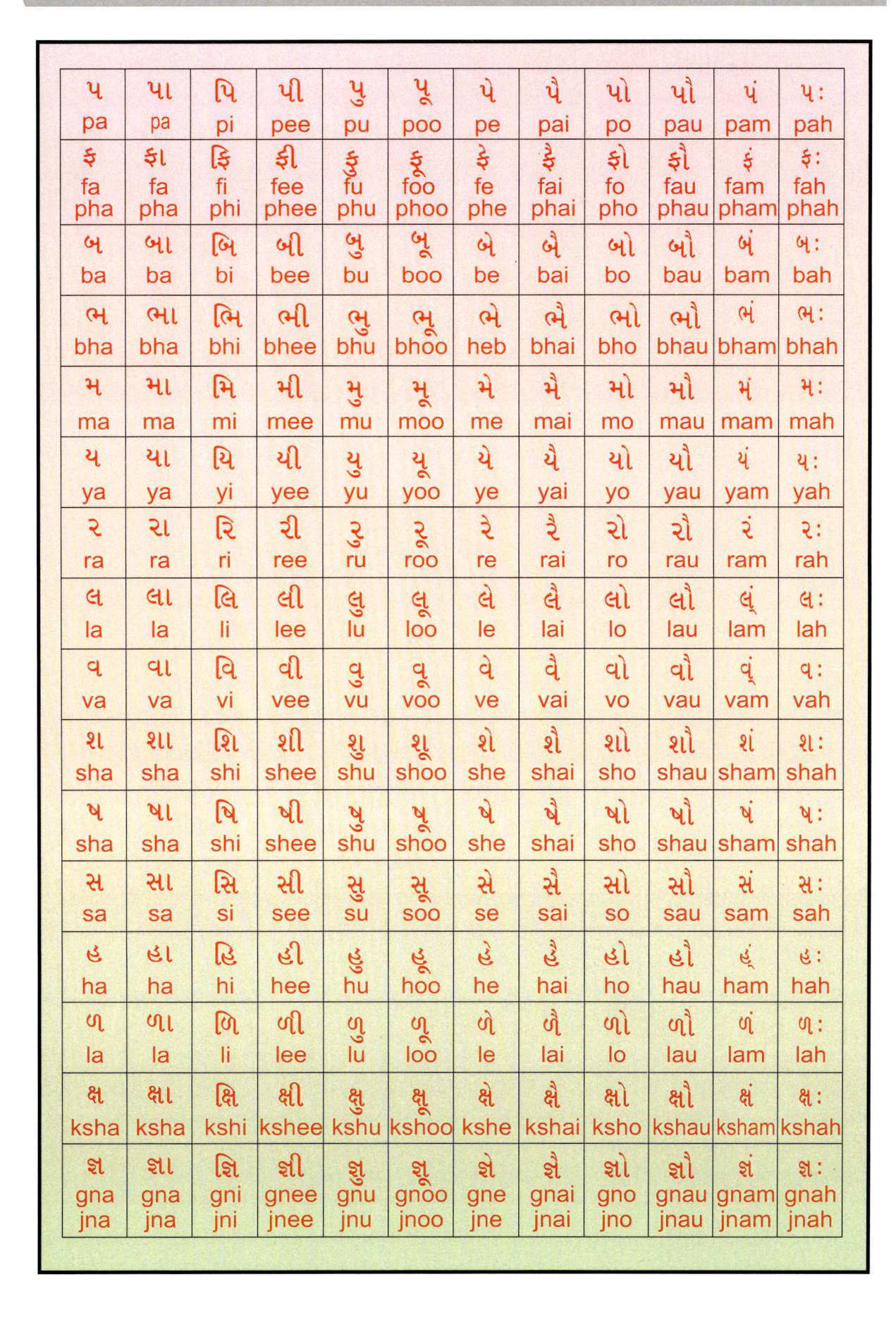

પ pa	પા pa	પિ pi	પી pee	પુ pu	પૂ poo	પે pe	પૈ pai	પો po	પૌ pau	પં pam	પઃ pah
ફ fa pha	ફા fa pha	ફિ fi phi	ફી fee phee	ફુ fu phu	ફૂ foo phoo	ફે fe phe	ફૈ fai phai	ફો fo pho	ફૌ fau phau	ફં fam pham	ફઃ fah phah
બ ba	બા ba	બિ bi	બી bee	બુ bu	બૂ boo	બે be	બૈ bai	બો bo	બૌ bau	બં bam	બઃ bah
ભ bha	ભા bha	ભિ bhi	ભી bhee	ભુ bhu	ભૂ bhoo	ભે heb	ભૈ bhai	ભો bho	ભૌ bhau	ભં bham	ભઃ bhah
મ ma	મા ma	મિ mi	મી mee	મુ mu	મૂ moo	મે me	મૈ mai	મો mo	મૌ mau	મં mam	મઃ mah
ય ya	યા ya	યિ yi	યી yee	યુ yu	યૂ yoo	યે ye	યૈ yai	યો yo	યૌ yau	યં yam	યઃ yah
ર ra	રા ra	રિ ri	રી ree	રુ ru	રૂ roo	રે re	રૈ rai	રો ro	રૌ rau	રં ram	રઃ rah
લ la	લા la	લિ li	લી lee	લુ lu	લૂ loo	લે le	લૈ lai	લો lo	લૌ lau	લં lam	લઃ lah
વ va	વા va	વિ vi	વી vee	વુ vu	વૂ voo	વે ve	વૈ vai	વો vo	વૌ vau	વં vam	વઃ vah
શ sha	શા sha	શિ shi	શી shee	શુ shu	શૂ shoo	શે she	શૈ shai	શો sho	શૌ shau	શં sham	શઃ shah
ષ sha	ષા sha	ષિ shi	ષી shee	ષુ shu	ષૂ shoo	ષે she	ષૈ shai	ષો sho	ષૌ shau	ષં sham	ષઃ shah
સ sa	સા sa	સિ si	સી see	સુ su	સૂ soo	સે se	સૈ sai	સો so	સૌ sau	સં sam	સઃ sah
હ ha	હા ha	હિ hi	હી hee	હુ hu	હૂ hoo	હે he	હૈ hai	હો ho	હૌ hau	હં ham	હઃ hah
ળ la	ળા la	ળિ li	ળી lee	ળુ lu	ળૂ loo	ળે le	ળૈ lai	ળો lo	ળૌ lau	ળં lam	ળઃ lah
ક્ષ ksha	ક્ષા ksha	ક્ષિ kshi	ક્ષી kshee	ક્ષુ kshu	ક્ષૂ kshoo	ક્ષે kshe	ક્ષૈ kshai	ક્ષો ksho	ક્ષૌ kshau	ક્ષં ksham	ક્ષઃ kshah
જ્ઞ gna jna	જ્ઞા gna jna	જ્ઞિ gni jni	જ્ઞી gnee jnee	જ્ઞુ gnu jnu	જ્ઞૂ gnoo jnoo	જ્ઞે gne jne	જ્ઞૈ gnai jnai	જ્ઞો gno jno	જ્ઞૌ gnau jnau	જ્ઞં gnam jnam	જ્ઞઃ gnah jnah

Chapter - 1

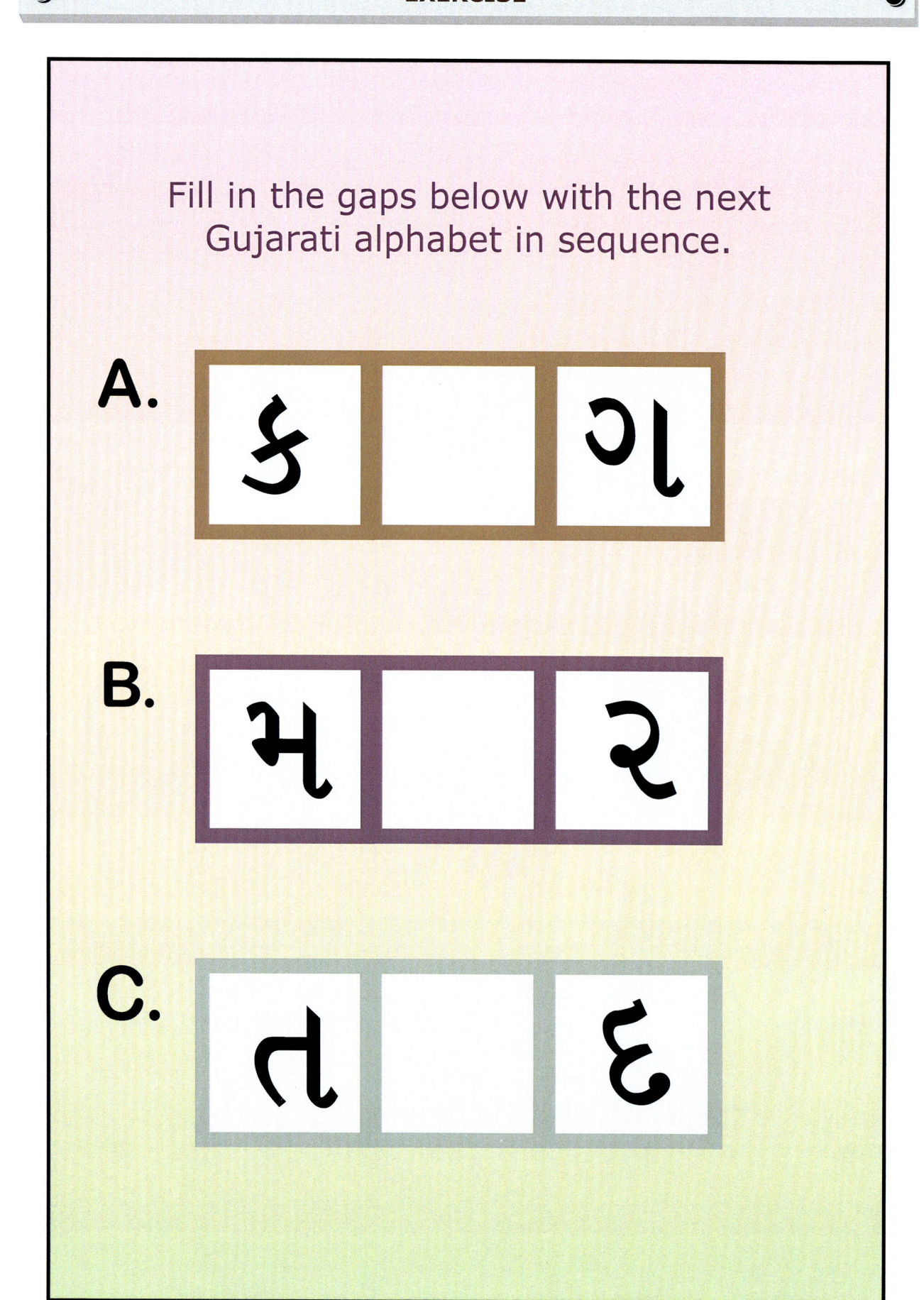

EXERCISE

Fill in the gaps below with the next Gujarati alphabet in sequence.

A. | ક | | ગ |

B. | મ | | ર |

C. | ત | | દ |

CHAPTER - 2

PARTS OF THE BODY - SHARIR NA ANGO - શરીર ના અંગો

HEAD - MATHU - માથું

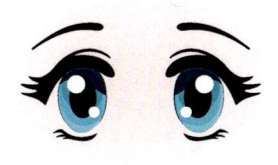

EYES - ANKHO - આંખો

NOSE - NAAK - નાક

CHEEK - GAAL - ગાલ

LIPS - HOTH - હોઠ
HOT - હોઠ

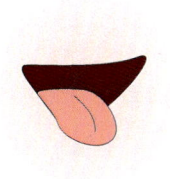

TONGUE - JIBH - જીભ

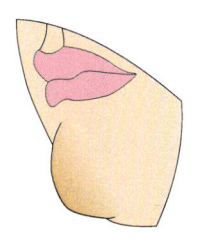

CHIN - DADHI - દાઢી

MOUTH - MODHU - મોઢું

FACE - CHAHERO - ચહેરો

HAIR - VAAL - વાળ
VAAR - વાર

Chapter - 2

PARTS OF THE BODY - SHARIR NA ANGO - શરીર ના અંગો

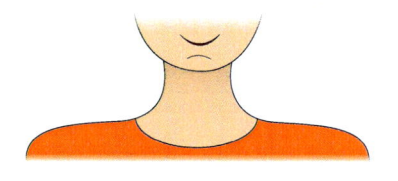

NECK - GADU - ગળું
GARU - ગરુ

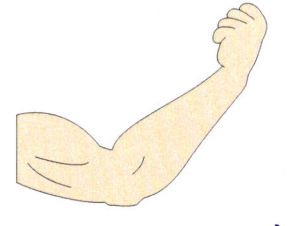

ELBOW - KONI - કોણી

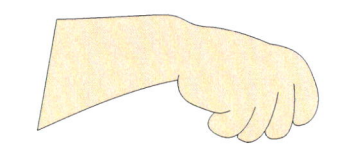

WRIST - KANDU - કાંડુ

THUMB - ANGUTHO - અંગુઠો
ANGUTO - અંગુઠો

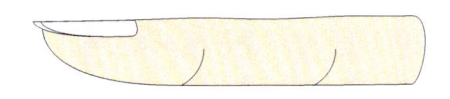

FINGER - ANGADI - આંગળી
ANGARI - આંગરી

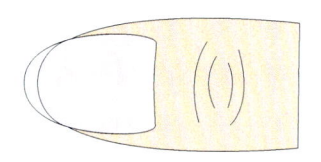

NAIL - NAKH - નખ

HAND - HATH - હાથ

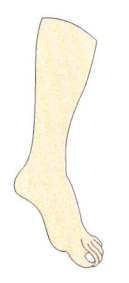

FOOT - PAG - પગ

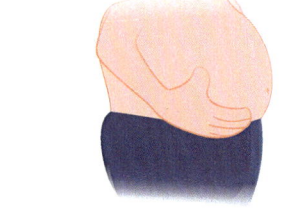

STOMACH - PET - પેટ

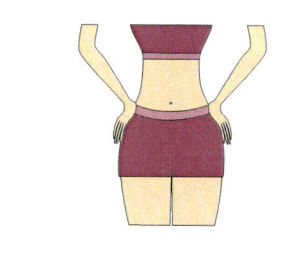

WAIST - KAMAR - કમર

Chapter - 2

EXERCISE

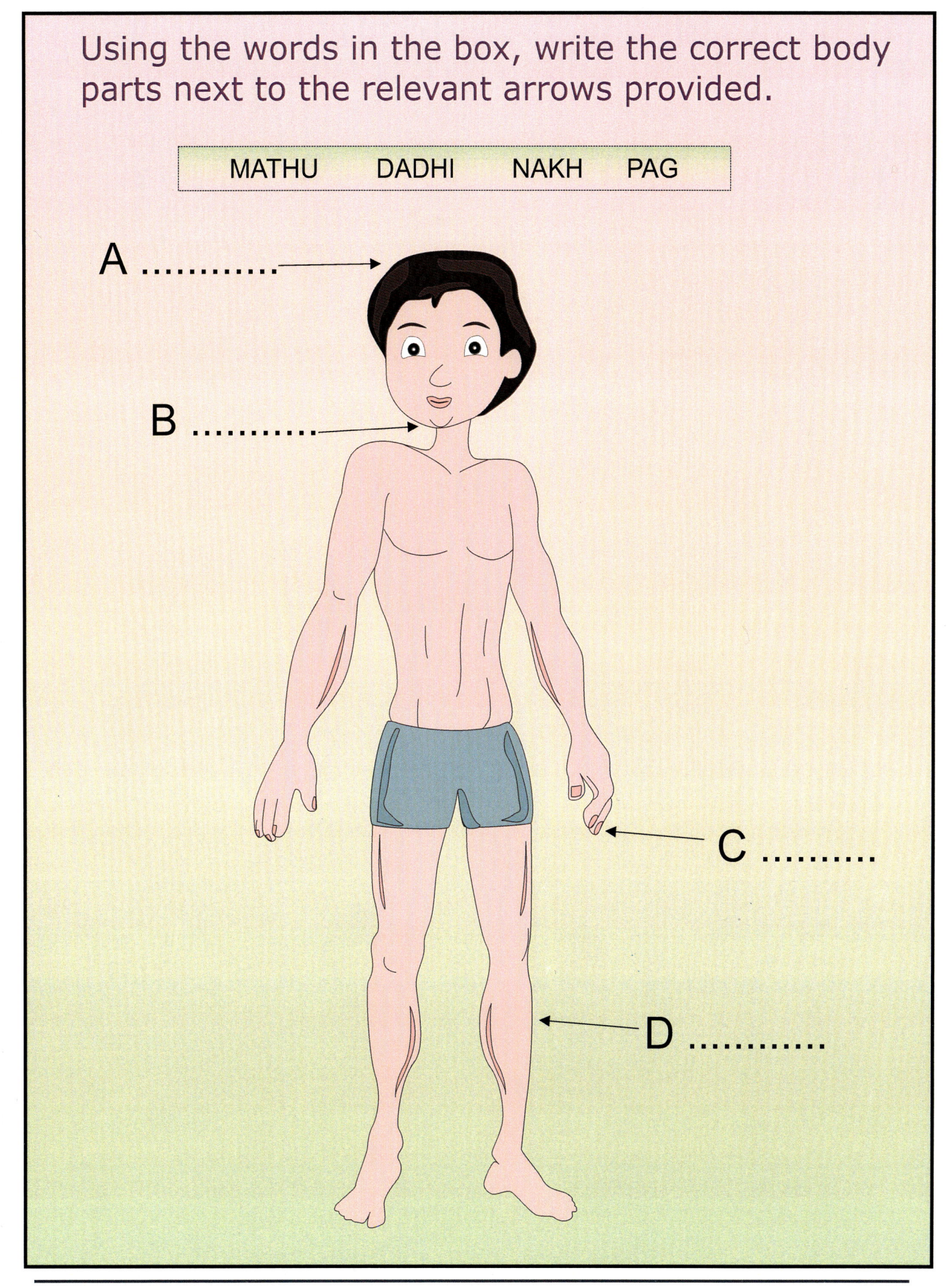

Using the words in the box, write the correct body parts next to the relevant arrows provided.

| MATHU | DADHI | NAKH | PAG |

A ....

B ....

C ....

D ....

Page 11

CHAPTER - 3

MY FAMILY - MARU KUTUMB - મારું કુટુંબ

I/ME/MYSELF - HUN - હું

I AM A BOY.

HUN CHOKARO CHHU.

હું છોકરો છું.

I AM A GIRL.

HUN CHOKARI CHHU.

હું છોકરી છું.

MY NAME IS………………………

MARU NAAM………………CHHE.

મારું નામ ………………છે.

THIS IS MY FAMILY.

AA MARU FAMILY / KUTUMB CHHE.

આ મારું ફેમિલી / કુટુંબ છે.

BROTHER - ભાઈ

THIS IS MY BROTHER.

AA MARO BHAI CHHE.

આ મારો ભાઈ છે.

SISTER - બેન

THIS IS MY SISTER.

AA MARI BEN CHHE.

આ મારી બેન છે.

Chapter - 3

MY FAMILY - MARU KUTUMB - મારું કુટુંબ

DAD - પપ્પા
THIS IS MY DAD.
AA MARA PAPA CHHE.
આ મારા પપ્પા છે.

MUM - મમ્મી
THIS IS MY MUM.
AA MARA MUMMY CHHE.
આ મારા મમ્મી છે.

GRANDFATHER - દાદા
THIS IS MY GRANDFATHER.
AA MARA DADA CHHE.
આ મારા દાદા છે.

GRANDMOTHER - દાદી
THIS IS MY GRANDMOTHER.
AA MARA DADI CHHE.
આ મારા દાદી છે.

MOTHER'S FATHER - NANA - નાના

MOTHER'S MOTHER - NANI - નાની

ADA - અદા
FATHER'S ELDEST BROTHER

BHABHU - ભાભુ
HIS WIFE

Chapter - 3

MY FAMILY - MARU KUTUMB - મારું કુટુંબ

KAKA - કાકા
FATHER'S YOUNGER BROTHER

KAKI - કાકી
HIS WIFE

MAMA - મામા
MOTHER'S BROTHER

MAMI - મામી
HIS WIFE

MASI - માસી
MOTHER'S SISTER

MASA - માસા
HER HUSBAND

Chapter - 3

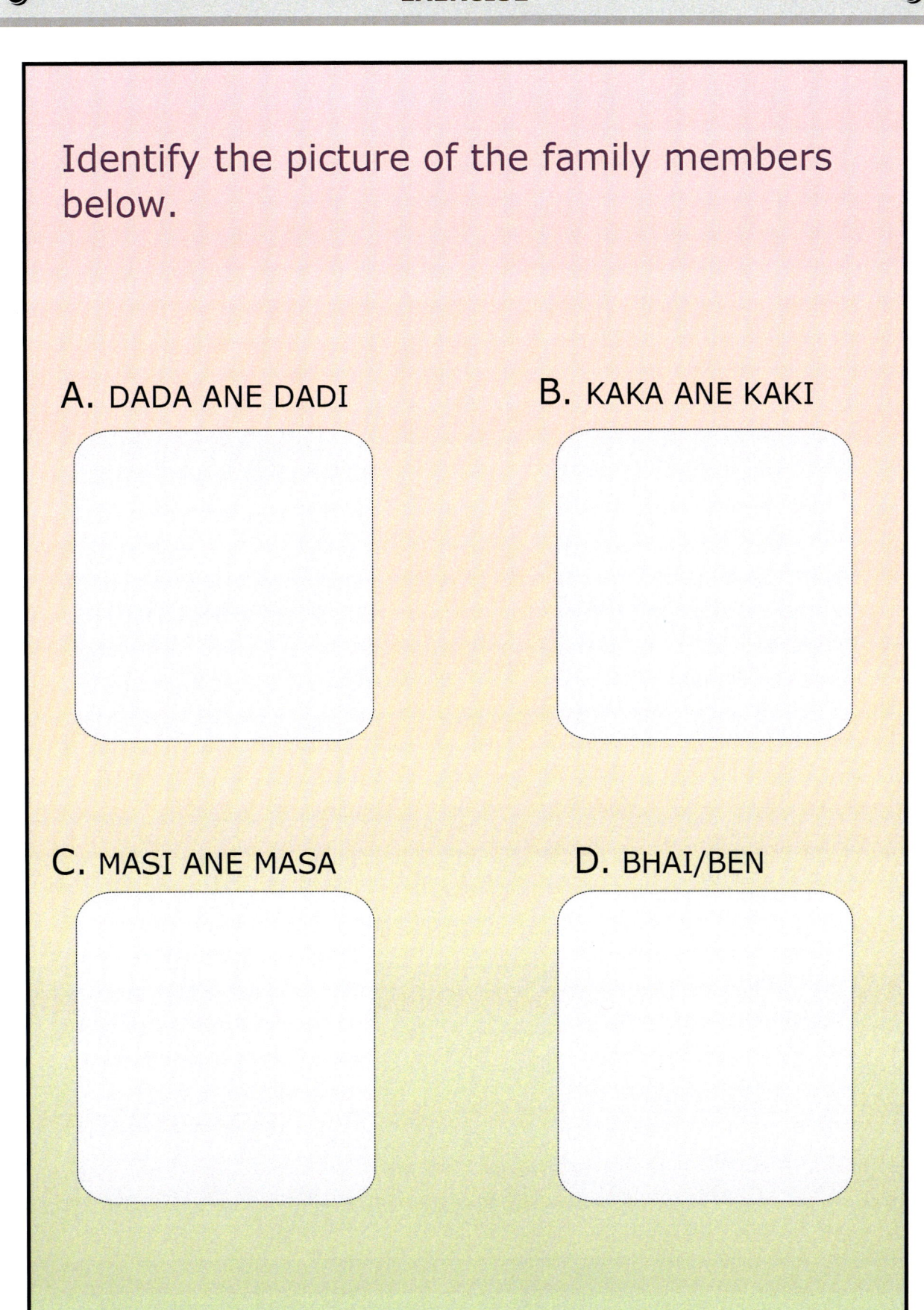

EXERCISE

Identify the picture of the family members below.

A. DADA ANE DADI

B. KAKA ANE KAKI

C. MASI ANE MASA

D. BHAI/BEN

Page 15

CHAPTER - 4 MY HOUSE - MARU GHAR – મારું ઘર

LIVING ROOM - BETHAK KHAND – બેઠક ખંડ

1. WINDOW - BAARI - બારી

2. FAN - PANKHO - પંખો

3. CLOCK - GHADIYAL - ઘડિયાળ
   GHARIYAR - ઘરિયાર

4. DOOR - DARWAJO - દરવાજો

5. PICTURE - CHITR - ચિત્ર

6. CURTAINS - PADADAA - પડદા
   PARDAA - પરદા

7. BOOK - PUSTAK - પુસ્તક

8. BOOK SHELF - PUSTAK KHANU - પુસ્તક ખાનુ

9. CHAIR - KHURSHI - ખુરશી

10. RUBBISH - KACHARO - કચરો

11. RUBBISH BIN - KACHARA PETI - કચરા પેટી

Page 16

Chapter - 4

KITCHEN - RASODU - રસોડું

1. WHEAT FLOUR - GHAU NO LOT - ઘઉં નો લોટ

2. GRAM FLOUR - CHANA NO LOT - ચણા નો લોટ

3. RICE (UN-COOKED) - CHOKHA - ચોખા

4. TURMERIC - HAL-DAR - હળદળ
   HAR-DAR - હરદર

5. CHILLI POWDER - MARACHA POWDER - મરચા પાવડર

6. CUMIN POWDER - JEERA POWDER - જીરા પાવડર

7. CORIANDER POWDER - DHANA POWDER - ધાણા પાવડર

8. SALT - NAMAK - નમક
   MITHU - મીઠું

9. BLACK PEPPER POWDER - MARI POWDER - મરી પાવડર

10. SPOON - CHAMACHI - ચમચી

11. KNIFE - CHARI - છરી

12. CUP-SAUCER - CUP-RAKABI - કપ-રકાબી

13. SUGAR - KHAND - ખાંડ

14. TEA BAG - CHANI PADIKI - ચા ની પડીકી

15. RICE (COOKED) - BHAT - ભાત

16. MATCHES - DIWASADI - દિવાસળી
    DIWASARI - દિવાસરી

17. POT - VASAN - વાસણ

18. ROLLING PIN - VELAN - વેલણ

19. DISH - THADI - થાળી
    THARI - થારી

Page 17

Chapter - 4

BED ROOM - SHAYAN KHAND - શયન ખંડ

1. PILLOW - OSHIKU - ઓશિકું

2. MATTRESS - GADLU - ગાદલું

3. BED - KHATLO - ખાટલો

4. BLANKET - RAJAI - રજાઈ

5. CUPBOARD - KABAT - કબાટ

6. CANDLE - MINBATTI - મીણબત્તી

7. SHOES RACK - JUTTA NU KHANU - જુતા નુ ખાનુ

8. SHOES - JUTTA - જુતા

9. CLOTHES - KAPDA - કપડા
    KAPRA - કપરા

10. SANDLES - CHAMPAL - ચંપલ

11. BED SHEET - CHAADAR - ચાદર

Chapter - 4

BATHROOM - SNANGHAR - સ્નાનઘર

1. MIRROR - ARISO - અરીસો

2. SOAP - SABU - સાબુ

3. COMB - DANTIYO - દાંતિયો

4. TOUNGE CLEANER - ULIYU - ઊલીયુ

5. MAT - PAG LUCHANIYU - પગ લૂછણિયું

6. TOWEL - TUVAL - ટુવાલ

7. TAP - NAD - નળ
   NAR - નર

8. WATER - PANI - પાણી

9. ROOF - CHAPRU - છાપરું

10. FLOOR - JAMEEN - જમીન

11. WALL - DIVAL - દીવાલ

Chapter - 4

GARDEN - BAGICHO - બગીચો

1. TREE - ZAAD - ઝાડ
   JHAR - જાર

2. FRUIT - PHAL - ફળ
   FAR - ફર

3. BRANCH - DADI - ડાળી
   DARI - ડારી

4. FLOWER - PHUL - ફૂલ

5. LEAF - PAN - પાન

6. FENCE - VAD - વાડ

7. ROOT - MUL - મૂળ
   MUR - મૂર

8. TRUNK - THAD - થડ

9. STONE - PATTHAR - પથ્થર

10. SEEDS - BI - બી

11. GRASS - GHAS - ઘાસ

12. CLIMBER - VEL - વેલ

13. PLANT - CHOD - છોડ
    CHOR - છોર

14. BUSHES - ZADI - ઝાડી
    JHARI - જારી

15. BUTTERFLY - PATANGIYU - પતંગિ

16. BEE - MADHMAKHI - મધમાખી

17. SWING - HINCHKO - હીંચકો

18. POT - KUNDU - કૂંડું

19. SOIL - MATI - માટી

20. FOUNTAIN - PHUVARO - ફુંવારો

21. SLIDE - LAPASANI - લપસણી

22. SAND - RETI - રેતી

Chapter - 4

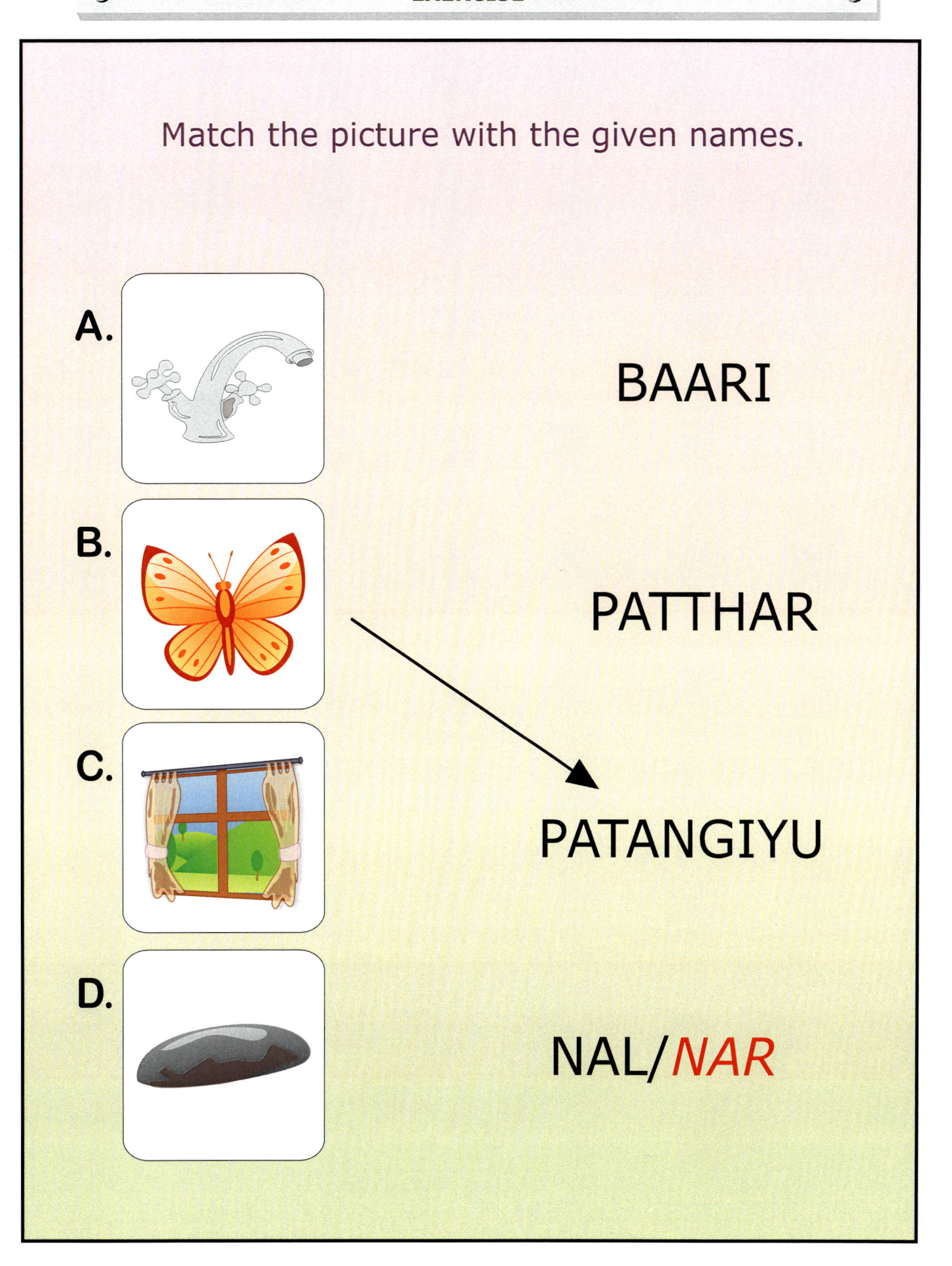

EXERCISE

Match the picture with the given names.

A. BAARI

B. PATTHAR

C. PATANGIYU

D. NAL/*NAR*

Page 21

CHAPTER - 5

1 TO 10 NUMBERS - EK THI DUS ANKDAO - ૧ થી ૧૦ આંકડાઓ

ONE - EK - એક
1 - ૧

TWO - BE - બે
2 - ૨

THREE - TRAN - ત્રણ
THRAN - ત્રન
3 - ૩

FOUR - CHAR - ચાર
4 - ૪

FIVE - PANCH - પાંચ
5 - ૫

SIX - CHA - છ
6 - ૬

Chapter - 5

1 TO 10 NUMBERS - EK THI DUS AKDAO - ૧ થી ૧૦ આંકડાઓ

SEVEN - SAAT - સાત
SATHA - સાત
7 - ૭

EIGHT - AATH - આઠ
AATA - આઠ
8 - ૮

NINE - NAV - નવ
9 - ૯

TEN - DAS - દસ
10 - ૧૦

Chapter - 5

EXERCISE

Fill in the gaps with the next Gujarati number in sequence.

A. | ૩ | | ૫ |

B. | ૭ | | ૯ |

C. | ૪ | | ૬ |

CHAPTER - 6

DAYS OF THE WEEK - ATHAVADIYU - અઠવાડિયું

MONDAY - SOMVAR - સોમવાર

TUESDAY - MANGALVAR - મંગળવાર
MANGARVAR - મંગરવાર

WEDNESDAY - BUDHAVAR - બુધવાર

THURSDAY - GURUVAR - ગુરુવાર

FRIDAY - SUKRAVAR - શુક્રવાર

SATURDAY - SHANIVAR - શનિવાર

SUNDAY - RAVIVAR - રવિવાર

Chapter - 6

TIME - SAMAY - સમય

ONE O'CLOCK - EK VAGYO - એક વાગ્યો

TWO O'CLOCK - BE VAGYA - બે વાગ્યા

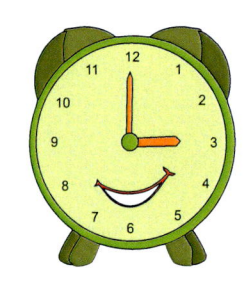

THREE O'CLOCK - TRAN VAGYA - ત્રણ વાગ્યા
THRAN VAGYA - ત્રન વાગ્યા

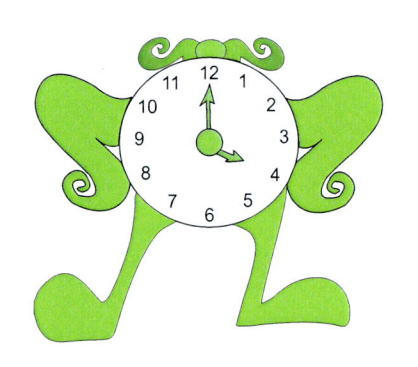

FOUR O'CLOCK - CHAR VAGYA - ચાર વાગ્યા

FIVE O'CLOCK - PANCH VAGYA - પાંચ વાગ્યા

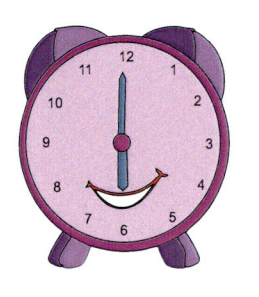

SIX O'CLOCK - CHA VAGYA - છ વાગ્યા

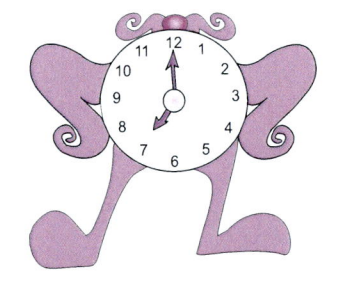

SEVEN O'CLOCK - SAAT VAGYA - સાત વાગ્યા
SATHA VAGYA - સાત વાગ્યા

EIGHT O'CLOCK - AATH VAGYA - આઠ વાગ્ય
AATA VAGYA - આઠ વાગ્ય

Chapter - 6

TIME - SAMAY - સમય

NINE O'CLOCK - NAV VAGYA - નવ વાગ્યા

TEN O'CLOCK - DAS VAGYA - દસ વાગ્યા

ELEVEN O'CLOCK - AGIYAR VAGYA - અગિયાર વાગ્યા

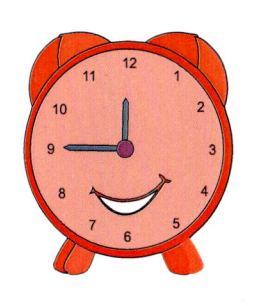

QUARTER TO TWELVE - PONA BAR VAGYA - પોણા બાર વાગ્યા

TWELVE O'CLOCK - BAAR VAGYA - બાર વાગ્યા

QUARTER PAST TWELVE - SAVA BAR VAGYA - સવાબાર વાગ્યા

HALF PAST TWELVE - SADA BAR VAGYA - સાડા બાર વાગ્યા
SARA BAR VAGYA - સારા બાર વાગ્યા

Chapter - 6

EXERCISE

Place a check mark next to the correct spelling.

A. SOMVAR ○ **OR** MOSVAR ○

B. VIARVAR ○ **OR** RAVIVAR ○

C. BUDHAVAR ○ **OR** DHBUVAR ○

Write the time in Gujarati below each clock.

D.

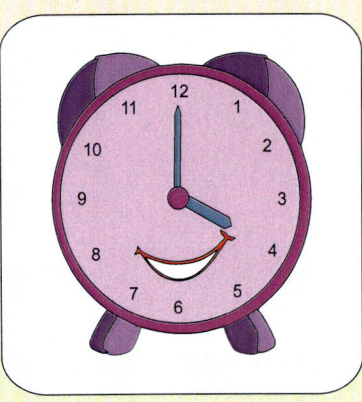

E.

F.

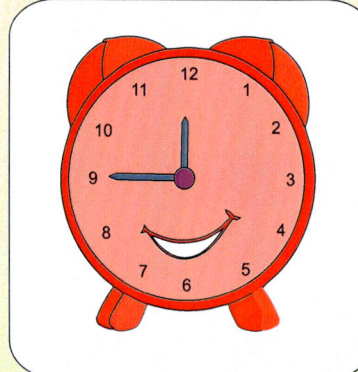

.... : .... : .... : ....

Page 28

CHAPTER - 7

SHAPES - AKAR - આકાર

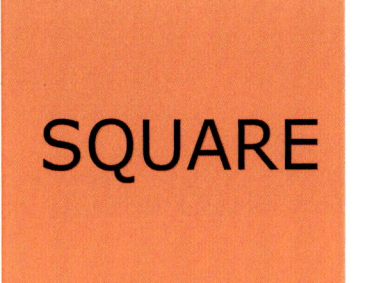

SQUARE — SQUARE - CHORAS - ચોરસ

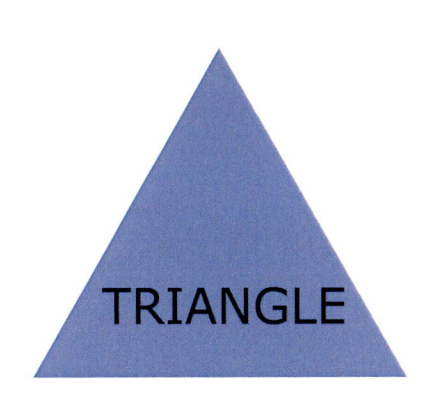

TRIANGLE — TRIANGLE - TRIKON - ત્રિકોણ

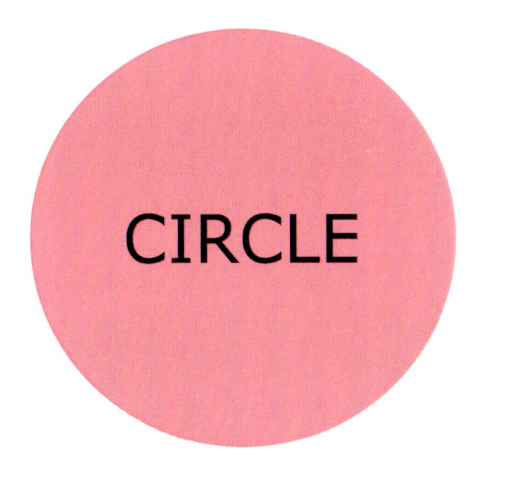

CIRCLE — CIRCLE - VARTUL - વર્તુળ
VARTUR - વર્તુર

RECTANGLE — RECTANGLE - LAMBCHORAS - લંબ ચોરસ

Chapter - 7

COLOURS - RANGO - રંગો

RED - LAL - લાલ

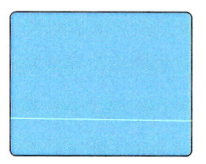

SKY - NILO - નીલો

ORANGE - KESARI - કેસરી

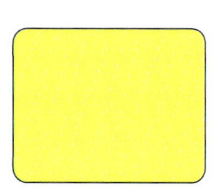

YELLOW - PILO - પીળો
PIRO - પીરો

BLUE - VADADI - વાદળી
VADARI - વાદરી

PINK - GULABI - ગુલાબી

GREEN - LILO - લીલો

PURPLE - JAMBLI - જાંબલી

BLACK - KADO - કાળો
KARO - કારો

WHITE - SAPHED - સફેદ

Chapter - 7

EXERCISE

Colour in each shape, using the information in the box.

LAL - △   PILO - ○   NILO - □   KESARI - ▭

Page 31

CHAPTER - 8

RELIGION AND FESTIVALS - DHARM ANE TAHEWARO - ધર્મ અને તહેવારો

HINDU - હિન્દુ

TEMPLE - MANDIR - મંદિર

UTTARAYAN - ઉત્તરાયણ/ઉત્તરાણ

HOLI - HODI - હોળી
HORI - હોરી

Chapter - 8

RELIGION AND FESTIVALS - DHARM ANE TAHEWARO - ધર્મ અને તહેવારો

RAKSHA-BANDHAN - રક્ષાબંધન

JANMASHTAMI - જન્માષ્ટમી

NAVARATRI - નવરાત્રી

DASHERA - દશેરા

Chapter - 8

● RELIGION AND FESTIVALS - DHARM ANE TAHEWARO - ધર્મ અને તહેવારો ●

DIWALI - DIWADI - દિવાળી
DIWARI - દિવારી

NEW YEAR - BESTU VARSH - બેસતુ વર્ષ

MUSLIM - મુસ્લિમ

MOSQUE - MASJID - મસ્જિદ

Chapter - 8

RELIGION AND FESTIVALS - DHARM ANE TAHEWARO - ધર્મ અને તહેવારો

EID - ઈદ

CHRISTIAN - KHRISTI - ખ્રિસ્તી

CHURCH - DEVAL - દેવળ
DEVAR - દેવર

CHRISTMAS - NATAL - નાતાલ

Page 35

Chapter - 8

EXERCISE

Answer the following questions in Gujarati.

A. In which Hindu festival would you fly kites?

Answer. ....

B. The dance of Garba is part of which festival?

Answer. ....

C. In which festival would you find Santa Clause?

Answer. ....

D. Which festival celebrates the birthday of Lord Krishna?

Answer. ....

EXERCISE

CHAPTER - 9

VEGETABLES AND FRUITS - SHAAKBHAJI ANE FADO - શાકભાજી અને ફળો

OKRA - BHINDA - ભીંડા

CUCUMBER - KAKADI - કાકડી
KAKRI - કાકરી

CAULIFLOWER - FULGOBI - ફૂલગોબી

GINGER - AADU - આદું

BITTER GOURD - KARELU - કારેલું

TOMATO - TAMETU - ટમેટું

CHILLI - MARCHU - મરચું

POTATO - BATETU - બટેટું

Chapter - 9

● VEGETABLES AND FRUITS - SHAAKBHAJI ANE FADO - શાકભાજી અને ફળો ●

CARROT - GAJAR - ગાજર

AUBERGINE - RINGADOO - રીંગણું
RINGAROO - રીંગરું

CORIANDER - KOTHMIR - કોથમીર

SPINACH - PALAK - પાલક

ONION - DUNGALI - ડુંગળી
DUNGARI - ડુંગરી

GARLIC - LASAN - લસણ

GUAVA - JAMPHAL - જામફળ
JAMPHAR - જામફર

ORANGE - NARANGI - નારંગી

Chapter - 9

● VEGETABLES AND FRUITS - SHAAKBHAJI ANE FADO - શાકભાજી અને ફળો ●

PAPAYA - PAPAIYU - પપૈયુ

APPLE - SAPHARAJAN - સફરજન

BANANA - KELU - કેળું
KERU - કેરુ

GRAPES - DRAKSH - દ્રાક્ષ

WATERMELON - TARABUCH - તરબૂચ

PINEAPPLE - ANANAS - અનાનસ

POMEGRANATE - DADAM - દાડમ
DARAM - દારમ

MANGO - KERI - કેરી

Page 39

Chapter - 9

EXERCISE

Write the name of each vegetable and fruit in Gujarati.

A. ....

B. ....

C. ....

D. ....

CHAPTER - 10

INDIAN FOOD - BHARTIY KHORAK - ભારતીય ખોરાક

BHAKHARI - ભાખરી

THEPLU - થેપલુ
(*Thepla* - થેપલા *for more than one*)

ROTALO - રોટલો
(*Rotla* - રોટલા *for more than one*)

ROTALI - રોટલી

PURI - પુરી

PAROTHU - પરોઠું
PAROTU - પરોઠું
(*Parotha* - પરોઠા *for more than one*)

MILK - DUDH - દૂધ

TEA - CHA - ચા

Page 41

Chapter - 10

INDIAN FOOD - BHARTIY KHORAK - ભારતીય ખોરાક

BUTTER - GHEE - ઘી

SWEET - MITHAI - મીઠાઈ
MITAI - મીઠાઈ

MANGO PULP - KERI NO RAS - કેરી નો રસ

PICKLE - ATHANU - અથાણું

KHICHADI - ખિચડી
KICHARI - ખિચરી

CHUTNEY - ચટણી

CURRY - SHAAK - શાક

DAAL - દાલ
DAAR - દાર

Page 42

Chapter -10

EXERCISE

Write the name of each food item in Gujarati.

A.  ....

B.  ....

C.  ....

D. ....

CHAPTER - 11

ANIMALS AND BIRDS - PRANIO ANE PAKSHIO - પ્રાણીઓ અને પક્ષીઓ

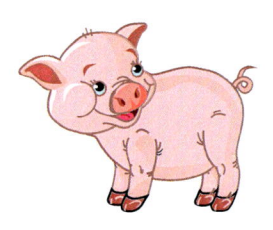

PIG - DUKKAR - ડુક્કર

SHEEP - GHETU - ઘેટું

RABBIT - SASALU - સસલું

FISH - MACHALI - માછલી

CAT - BILADI - બિલાડી
BILARI - બિલારી

TIGER - VAGH - વાઘ

MONKEY - VANDRO - વાંદરો

DOG - KUTARO - કૂતરો

FOX - SHIYAL - શિયાળ
SHIYAR - શિયાર

PIGEON - KABUTAR - કબૂતર

Chapter - 11

● ANIMALS AND BIRDS - PRANIO ANE PAKSHIO - પ્રાણીઓ અને પક્ષીઓ ●

COW - GAAY - ગાય

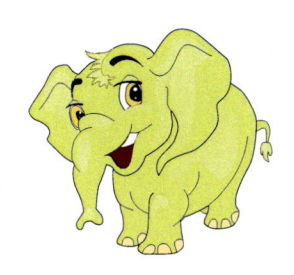

ELEPHANT - HATHI - હાથી

MOUSE - UNDAR - ઉંદર

CROW - KAGADO - કાગડો
KAGARO - કાગરો

PARROT - POPAT - પોપટ

CHICKEN - KUKADO - કુકડો
CUKARO - કુકરો

DUCK - BATAK - બતક
BATHAK - બતક

DONKEY - GADHEDO - ગધેડો
GADHERO - ગધેરો

HORSE - GHODO - ઘોડો
GHORO - ઘોરો

STORK - BA-GALO - બગલો

Page 45

Chapter - 11

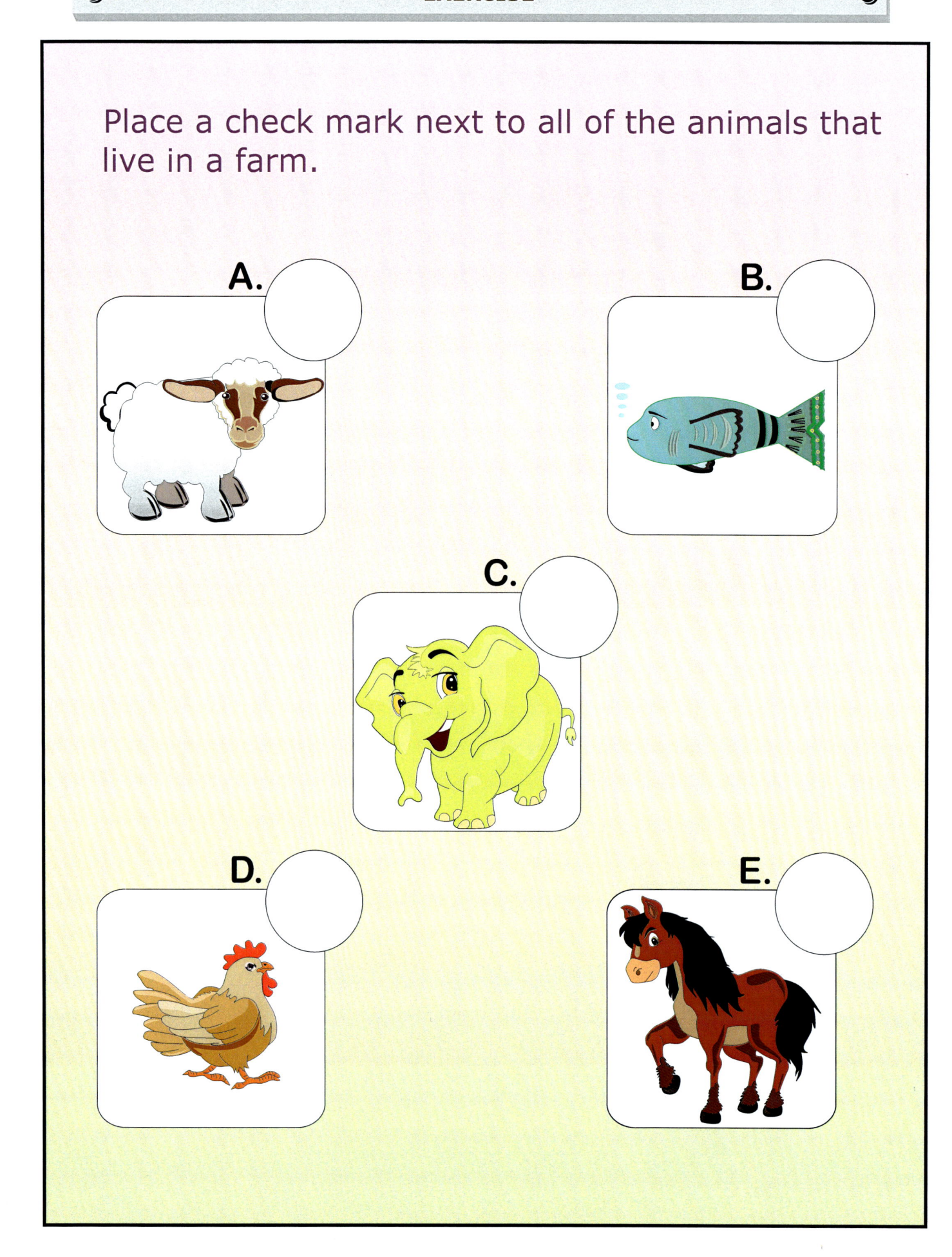

EXERCISE

Place a check mark next to all of the animals that live in a farm.

A.

B.

C.

D.

E.

CHAPTER - 12

NATURE AND WEATHER - KUDARAT ANE HAWAAMAN - કુદરત અને હવામાન

STARS - TARAO - તારાઓ

SUN - SURAJ - સૂરજ

MOON - CHANDO - ચાંદો

RAINBOW - MEGHDHANUSHYA - મેઘધનુષ્ય

WIND/BREEZE - HAVA - હવા

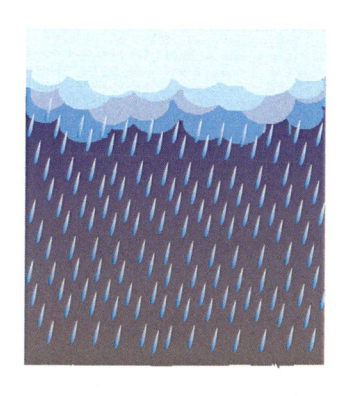

RAIN - VARASAD - વરસાદ

Chapter - 12

NATURE AND WEATHER - KUDARAT ANE HAWAAMAN - કુદરત અને હવામાન

ISLAND - TAPU - ટાપુ

VOLCANO - JWALAMUKHI - જ્વાળામુખી

LAKE - SAROWAR - સરોવર

WAVES - MOJA - મોજા

SEA - SAMUDRA - સમુદ્ર

RIVER - NADI - નદી

Page 48

Chapter -12

EXERCISE

Colour in the picture below and write the place of interest in Gujarati.

Place of Interest

....

Page 49

CHAPTER - 13

OPPOSITES - VIRUDHAARTHI - વિરુદ્ધાર્થી

OPEN - KHULLU - ખુલ્લુ

CLOSE - BANDH - બંધ

FAT - JADU - જાડુ

SLIM - PATALU - પાતળું
PATARU - પાતરુ

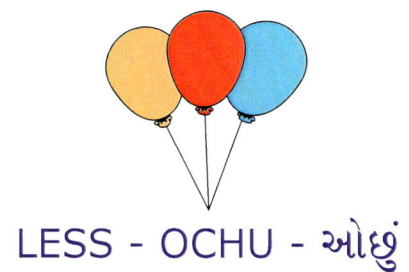

MORE - VAD-HA-RE - વધારે

LESS - OCHU - ઓછું

SHORT - TUKKU - ટૂંકું

LONG - LAMBU - લાંબું

Chapter - 13

OPPOSITES - VIRUDHAARTHI - વિરુધ્ધાર્થી

TALL - UNCHU - ઊંચું

SHORT - NICHU - નીચું

NEAR - NAJIK - નજીક

FAR - DUR - દૂર

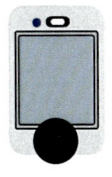

NEW - NAVU - નવું

OLD - JUNU - જૂનું

SWEET - GALYU - ગળ્યું

BITTER - KADAVU - કડવું
KARVU - કરવું

Page 51

Chapter - 13

OPPOSITES - VIRURDHARTHI - વિરુદ્ધાર્થી

BIG - MOTU - મોટું

SMALL - NANU - નાનું

CLEAN - SAAF - સાફ

DIRTY - GANDU - ગંદુ

HAPPY - SUKHI - સુખી

SAD - DUKHI - દુઃખી

LAUGH - HASWU - હસવું

CRY - RADWU - રડવું
RARWU - રરવું

Page 52

Chapter - 14

DAILY ACTIONS - DAR-ROJ NI KRIYAO - દરરોજ ની ક્રિયાઓ

RUN - DODAVU - દોડવું
DORVU - દોરવું

SHOOTING - GODIBAR - ગોળીબાર
GORIBAR - ગોરીબાર

SIT - BESAVU - બેસવું

WRITE - LAKHAVU - લખવું

SHOUT - BUM PADVI - બૂમ પાડવી
BUM PARVI - બૂમ પારવી

SING - GAVU - ગાવું

SLEEP - SUVU - સૂવું

SLIDE - SAR-AK-VU - સરકવું

TALK - VATCHIT - વાતચીત

THINK - VICHAR - વિચાર

Page 57

Chapter - 14

DAILY ACTIONS - DAR-ROJ NI KRIYAO - દરરોજ ની ક્રિયાઓ

SWEEP - VADVU - વાડવું
VAR-VU - વારવું

SWIM - TARAVU - તરવું

SMELL - SUNGHVU - સૂંઘવું

CALM - SHANT - શાંત

ANGRY - GUSSO KARVO - ગુસ્સો કરવો

SHY - SHARMAVU - શરમાવું

DEPRESSED - NIRASH THAVU - નિરાશ થવું

TALKATIVE - BOLAKU - બોલકું

SURPRISED - ASCHARY THAVU - આશ્ચર્ય થવું

LOVE - PREM - પ્રેમ

Page 58

Chapter -14

EXERCISE

Match the English words with the daily actions stated in Gujarati.

A. Read   Taravu

B. Sing   Ubha Rahevu

C. Sit   Vachavu

D. Stand   Gavu

E. Swim   Besvu

CHAPTER - 15

GUJARAT - ગુજરાત

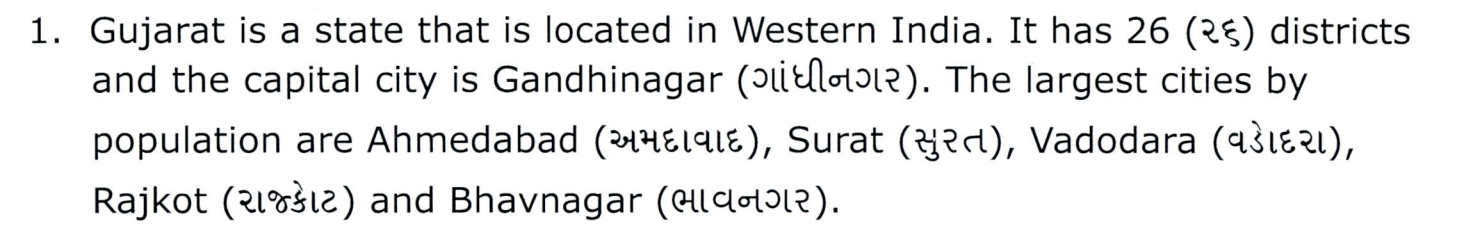

1. Gujarat is a state that is located in Western India. It has 26 (૨૬) districts and the capital city is Gandhinagar (ગાંધીનગર). The largest cities by population are Ahmedabad (અમદાવાદ), Surat (સુરત), Vadodara (વડોદરા), Rajkot (રાજકોટ) and Bhavnagar (ભાવનગર).

2. The most common language spoken is Gujarati (ગુજરાતી).

3. Mahatma Gandhi (મહાત્મા ગાંધી) who is considered as India's 'Father of the nation', was also Gujarati. He led the Indian independence movement against the British colonial rule.

4. There are more than 1000 (૧૦૦૦) festivals celebrated in this state.

5. Gujarat's film (ફિલ્મ) industry, is one of the largest regional and vernacular film industries of India.

6. Gujarati cuisine is primarily vegetarian and follows the traditional Indian full meal structure of rice (bhat-ભાત), cooked Vegetables (શાકભાજી), daal (દાળ) and roti (રોટલી).

7. The following items make up a typical Gujarati female attire: Mangalsutra (મંગળસુત્ર - Only worn by married females), bindi (બિંદી), necklace (har - હાર), nose ring (natha - નથ), ear-rings (kadi - કડી) and bangles (bangadi - બંગડી).

Symbols of Gujarat

- Animal - Lion - Sinha - સિંહ
- Dance - Garba - ગરબા
- Flower - Marigold - Galgoto - ગલગોટો
- Language - Gujarati - ગુજરાતી
- Sport - Cricket, Kabaddi - ક્રિકેટ, કબડ્ડી
- Fruit - Mango - Keri - કેરી

Chapter - 15

EXERCISE

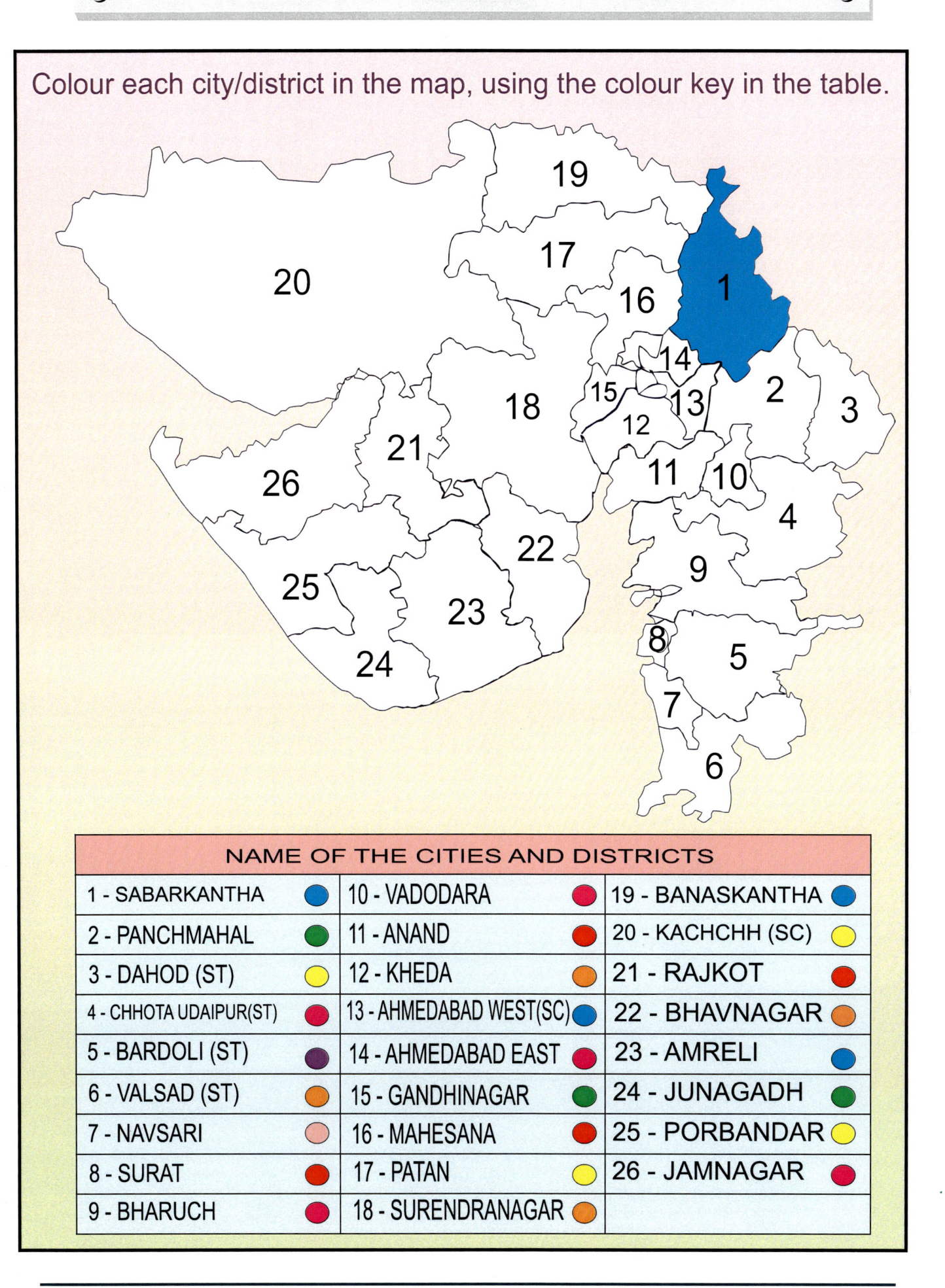

Colour each city/district in the map, using the colour key in the table.

NAME OF THE CITIES AND DISTRICTS					
1 - SABARKANTHA	🔵	10 - VADODARA	🔴	19 - BANASKANTHA	🔵
2 - PANCHMAHAL	🟢	11 - ANAND	🔴	20 - KACHCHH (SC)	🟡
3 - DAHOD (ST)	🟡	12 - KHEDA	🟠	21 - RAJKOT	🔴
4 - CHHOTA UDAIPUR(ST)	🔴	13 - AHMEDABAD WEST(SC)	🔵	22 - BHAVNAGAR	🟠
5 - BARDOLI (ST)	🟣	14 - AHMEDABAD EAST	🔴	23 - AMRELI	🔵
6 - VALSAD (ST)	🟠	15 - GANDHINAGAR	🟢	24 - JUNAGADH	🟢
7 - NAVSARI	🌸	16 - MAHESANA	🔴	25 - PORBANDAR	🟡
8 - SURAT	🔴	17 - PATAN	🟡	26 - JAMNAGAR	🔴
9 - BHARUCH	🔴	18 - SURENDRANAGAR	🟠		

ANSWER KEY

Chapter 1   A - ૫, B - ૫, C - ૩.

Chapter 2   A - Mathu, B - Dadhi, C - Nakh, D - Pag.

Chapter 3   Identify the picture of the family members, shown in pages 12,13 and 14.

Chapter 4   A - Nad/*Nar*, B - Patangiyu, C - Baari, D - Patthar.

Chapter 5   A - ૪, B - ૮, C - ૫.

Chapter 6   A - Somvar, B - Ravivar, C - Budhavar,
D - ૪:૦૦, E - ૭:૦૦, F - ૧૧:૪૫.

Chapter 7   Red - Triangle, Yellow - Circle, Blue - Square, Orange - Rectangle.

Chapter 8   A - Uttarayan, B - Navratri, C - Natal, D - Janmashtami.

Chapter 9   A - Gajar, B - Kakadi/*Kakri*, C - Keri, D - Kelu/*Keru.*

Chapter 10 A - Theplu, B - Khichadi/*Khichari*, C - Puri, D - Dudh.

Chapter 11 A, D, E.

Chapter 12 Sarowar.

Chapter 13 A - H, B - G, C - F, D - E.

Chapter 14 A - Vachavu, B - Gavu, C - Besavu, D - Ubha Rahevu, E - Taravu.

Chapter 15 Colour each city/district in the map, using the colour key in the table.